PET CAM

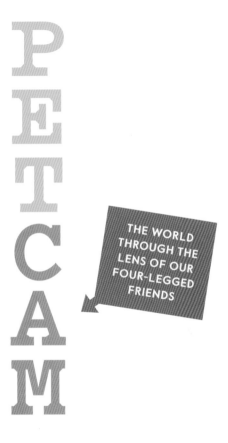

THE WORLD
THROUGH THE
LENS OF OUR
FOUR-LEGGED
FRIENDS

Chris Keeney

Princeton Architectural Press, New York

Published by
Princeton Architectural Press
37 East Seventh Street
New York, New York 10003

Visit our website at www.papress.com.

Editor: Sara Stemen
Designer: Elana Schlenker
Additional text: Jay Sacher

Special thanks to:
Meredith Baber, Sara Bader,
Nicola Bednarek Brower, Janet Behning,
Megan Carey, Carina Cha, Andrea Chlad,
Barbara Darko, Benjamin English,
Russell Fernandez, Will Foster,
Jan Hartman, Jan Haux, Diane Levinson,
Jennifer Lippert, Katharine Myers,
Jaime Nelson, Rob Shaeffer, Marielle Suba,
Kaymar Thomas, Paul Wagner, and
Joseph Weston of Princeton Architectural
Press —Kevin C. Lippert, publisher

Library of Congress Cataloging-in-
Publication Data is available from the
publisher upon request.

CONTENTS

INTRODUCTION

Ever since I was a child I've enjoyed the company of various pet friends, from the family golden retriever, Happy, to a chicken named Bee Beeps, who would run free around our house and yard and lay eggs in a big brass bucket we kept in our living room. Sometimes she would peck at strangers' socks if she thought they were too colorful. Her quirks were endearing, and I learned to love and care for pets as if they were my siblings. I often wondered where Bee Beeps would wander during the day and always hoped that she would come home safely to roost in her box.

Thanks to small, lightweight cameras that easily attach to collars or harnesses, we can now observe our beloved pets' daily routines and discover how they spend their time when they're out and about: napping under parked cars, climbing on rooftops, resting on porches, playing with sticks, staring at birdhouses, or jumping in the water. At a time when cell phones are equipped with high-quality camera lenses and capturing and sharing our daily

Pigeon fitted with a camera.

rituals has never been easier, it's not surprising that technology has also made it possible for animals to document their own experiences. This privileged glimpse into the lives of our pets and fellow creatures—at once so close and familiar to us, yet in many ways living among us as aliens—may open up strange new worlds and change forever the way we think about the lines between humans and animals. Like Alice down the rabbit hole, we may feel sometimes bewildered, often amused, and always enlightened as we view our surroundings through the fascinating perspectives of these intrepid canine, feline, or bovine explorers. We are certain to return transformed by the adventure.

The devices are new, but the impulse to give animals cameras is an old one. It turns out that pet photography has been around for a while: as early as 1908, in an effort to create aerial photographs from a bird's perspective, the German photographer and inventor Julius Gustav Neubronner patented a small camera that could be attached to passenger pigeons. Visitors to international exhibitions could watch as these camera-rigged pigeons made safe landings. Neubronner would then develop the film on the spot and would sell the resulting prints as souvenir postcards, satisfying spectators' curiosity about the bird's-eye view.

So how exactly does a dog or cat or cow or horse take a photo? A pet camera can be attached to an animal by clipping it to the bottom of a collar or by securing it to a harness. Some harnesses are specially designed with attachments that position the camera on the animal's back, which can capture a completely different perspective. These harnesses work best for larger animals.

I can't stress enough how important it is to carefully assess the weight of the camera in relationship to the size and weight of your pet. There are various small, light PetCams on the market, ones that an animal can carry on a collar with no stress or discomfort. But some animals, like our cat, Alice, have never worn a collar. It took Alice just a few unsupervised minutes to figure out a way to remove both the collar and the camera (although it took me two days to find both under the porch, where she left them). Even if your pet gets excited when the PetCam comes out of the drawer and is eager to wear it, be sure to remove the camera after each expedition, regardless of how light it is. It's our responsibility to ensure the safety, well-being, and happiness of our pets, and while our family dog, Fred, absolutely loves his camera, Alice is clearly not interested. She watches her brother take photos from the sidelines but doesn't participate herself. *Respecting your pet's response to the camera and the animal's comfort level is the single most important part of this process.*

PetCams can be programmed to snap pictures at specific time intervals (one-half second, one second, two, three...). Once you press the start button on the camera and your pet begins to explore, the device records images at the set interval and saves them to an internal memory card. When the memory card is full, the camera stops taking photos.

The act of creating something with an animal inevitably generates a bond. Essentially, you're collaborators. Setting off with a PetCam rigged to your pup's collar means that an adventure is in store for both of you. Whenever I attach the camera to Fred, he gets excited. He knows that we're about to go somewhere fun, often a place new to both of us. And since the camera is small, it doesn't get in the way of his good time or weigh him down as he explores.

After the two of you have returned from your adventure together, with that camera full of photographs, what do you do with all those photos? You'll sort through a bunch of, well, not-so-good snapshots to find a few stellar shots. In this digital age of photography we've become accustomed to taking dozens or even hundreds of photos, hoping for a few shining stars that will make our efforts worthwhile. In pet photography the law of averages is definitely working against you, but if you know that going in—and you're willing to keep at it—you will be well rewarded.

You may also find a new appreciation for those "not-so-good" shots, which may offer a texture you wouldn't have captured intentionally with your own camera. Even if they are somewhat blurry, they often are charming because they reveal an unexpected point of view.

As a pinhole photographer I've spent many years exploring the creative boundaries of experimental, do-it-yourself photography. One of the many reasons that pinhole photography has held my interest for so long is that I never know quite what I'm going to discover when I develop my negatives. I can choose the scene and pick a certain size and shape of pinhole camera—perhaps one made out of a matchbox, shoe box, or oatmeal cylinder—and I can select the film, but in the end, certain factors are always left to chance: the weather, the lighting, the movement of subjects. That element of surprise is an integral part of the process.

A similar sense of wonder is an essential part of the PetCam experience. When Fred and I head out on a shoot, I set his camera's frequency, but the rest is really up to him. What he wants to explore, how close he gets to the subject matter, how still he is when the camera fires off those shots—it's all part of the creative process. So when we return home and I load Fred's digital handiwork into the computer, my level of anticipation runs pretty high.

The photographs gathered in this collection—created by Fred and a talented international roster of pets large and small and described in what we might imagine as their own "voices"—have stopped me in my tracks: the perspective, movement, colors, details, choice of subjects, and humor. While I've felt a deep connection to animals for as far back as I can remember, collaborating with these creatures and the owners who love them has only heightened my appreciation for them. Seeing what they see has offered me a rare and wonderful glimpse into how our beloved friends experience and explore the world that we all share. I hope their photographs offer the same for you.

THE PHOTOGRAPHERS

ABBOTT

I came up hard on the streets of Pittsburgh, and the runaway aesthetic really informs my photography. Those shoes in my photos—are they going to kick you? Or will they simply be delicious once you sink your chompers into their Dr. Scholl's-y goodness? These are the hard questions I want my work to raise.

Now that I've moved to the country, my critics think I've gone soft. But I say they're a bunch of art-school jerks. Excuse me for wanting to take a nap in the garden, enjoy a bit of sunshine and maybe a cow chase now and again. Don't get me started on my critics. It raises my dang hackles.

Jack Russell Terrier
Bath, New York

PetCam

Shoes really are the cheesesteaks of the dog world. Well, I guess if we're being honest, cheesesteaks really are the cheesesteaks of the dog world, but we'll take what we can get.

 Abbott • Jack Russell Terrier

There's a vicious lie going around that dogs are color-blind. That's nonsense! But I admit that I was really drawn to the lovely shades of gray in this image.

Abbott • Jack Russell Terrier

ASTRO

I'm at the beach, or the beach is
at me, am I right? Gimme some sand,
surf, somebody's feet to sit on,
and some peanut butter in my belly,
and I got myself a perfect day. I'm a
scene stealer and a crowd pleaser.
My photos? They just kinda happen—
you can't force these things.

Chihuahua
San Diego,
California

Astro • Chihuahua

PetCam

Astro • Chihuahua

PetCam

I think there's a shark in this picture. If you squint, you totally see a dorsal fin. Yep, totally a shark. (I dunno, maybe I've been bingeing too much on Shark Week.)

Astro • Chihuahua

Sometimes I get pretty introspective, like I wonder: Can I count
all the grains of sand on this beach? But then I remember: I'm a dog,
and I can't count. I don't even know what sand *is*, dude.

 Astro • Chihuahua

BOTTY

Botty here, with my oh-so-dreary *statement d'artiste*. I do so love a good photograph: it should capture certain spirit, a certain *I don't know what*. I rather think I've got an eye for the quiet moments: a hint of sunlight through an open window or the rustic charm of suburban decay. Really, though, my muse is my sister, Miffy. She's a bit of a ruffian, to be honest, always toddling about under automobiles. I know it's warm under there, Miff, but what about your coat?

Domestic
Shorthair Cat
London, England

PetCam

Here's my sister, Miffy. I call this one "The Dullard Awaits." Poor Miff.

 Botty • Domestic Shorthair Cat

CASPER

I was the tiniest one in my litter, but do you think that means I'm slow-moving? Destined to be overlooked? Well, some dogs might stand for being called a "runt," but not me, not Casper from Germantown, no sir. You can call me an "alpha-runt." I appear and disappear like a friendly ghost, and I roll deep with the big boys. I started taking pictures early in my young life and have wowed all my dog friends and human companions with my photographic panache. Take a look. Go ahead and be wowed by a "runt."

Labrador Retriever
Germantown,
New York

Big dog may be jealous of my photo-taking chops, but that's not going to stop me from licking her face.

 PetCam

Casper • Labrador Retriever

C
H
I
C
K
E
N

My name is "Chicken" because,
frankly, it helps me remember
what I am. Nothing wrong with
that. I just get confused sometimes.
You see, I like to eat cat food.
That's my favorite treat. So I got to
thinking one day...maybe I'm a cat?
Maybe when I think I'm saying "cluck,"
I'm really saying "meow." It kind of
blew my mind. I freaked out. I ran
around like a chicken with its head...
well, you get the idea. So I turned to
art to help me solve this conundrum.
My photography reflects this
identity crisis. Critics have called
my work very "feline." I take that
as a great compliment.

Ameraucana
Chicken
Davis, California

PetCam

PetCam

Chicken   •   Ameraucana Chicken

PetCam

My sister Butthead: the huntress.

Chicken • Ameraucana Chicken

COULEE

Here in Canada we have wide-open spaces, no litter on our streets, a segment of our population that sort of speaks French, two-dollar coins, and the cultural legacy of SCTV. This all makes life pretty good, for humans and dogs alike. I think my pictures reflect that basic sense that everything is totally, amazingly cool.

Border Collie/
Golden Retriever
Mix

Lethbridge,
Alberta, Canada

PetCam

I'm giving these sheep the "bum's rush."

 Coulee • Border Collie/Golden Retriever Mix

My statement on the inevitability of geopolitical conflict.

Coulee • Border Collie/Golden Retriever Mix

Who doesn't get a thrill from
watching another creature clean
up your own poo? I'm holding on
to this one for blackmail purposes.

PetCam

FIDA & LOLA

It is a truth universally acknowledged, that a single cow in possession of a good camera must be in want of decent photographic subjects. If, however, you have two cows with cameras (like me and my BFF Lola), and if you happen to live in the Swiss Alps (which we do), well, it's a whole different story. We're getting all *Sound of Music* up in this piece.

Brown Swiss Cows
Val Müstair.
Switzerland

Can't you totally hear this picture? The gentle rustling
and snorting of us cows, the clanging of our dear little bells?
Just be glad you can't smell it.

Fida & Lola • Brown Swiss Cows

PetCam

Are we relaxing on the side of a mountain or is this start of a stampede? I don't remember. I was pretty drunk that day.

Fida & Lola • Brown Swiss Cows

FIONA

I'm not just taking postcard snaps over here. I'm creating lasting art. It's like I'm shooting a John Ford western. After you see my photos, I suggest just taking your camera, your prints, and your self-esteem and just dropping them down the toilet, because you cannot compare. No apologies here.

Red Angus Cow
San Diego,
California

PetCam

Fiona • Red Angus Cow

PetCam

Flying chicken. Yawn. I can fly, too.

 Fiona • Red Angus Cow

For a long time I thought this shed was our outhouse. But hey,
I'm a cow. I can go to the bathroom wherever I please.

Fiona   •   Red Angus Cow

This is Adrianna. She's an amateur tongue wrestler.

PetCam

FRED

Some people call me Fred, some people call me Fred-Fred, some people call me Freddie. That's the way it goes with humans—they have no sense of proportion, no sense of consistency. I know I don't have a job or anything like that, but I must say that I do like going on vacation. Just getting away from the grind of dogginess—you know what I mean. That's when I take my best pictures— when I can really zone out and focus.

Chihuahua/Terrier Mix

San Diego, California

PetCam

Fred   •   Chihuahua/Terrier Mix

I don't know why Walter is all up in my face, but it's terrifying.

Fred • Chihuahua/Terrier Mix

PetCam

Some dogs go for mailmen, others for cats. For me, it's the delicate ankles of adolescents. Can't get enough of 'em.

Fred • Chihuahua/Terrier Mix

Had a couple of pints while master wasn't looking.

Fred • Chihuahua/Terrier Mix

FRITZ

My body of work, begun at age two, addresses how postrelational aesthetics are absorbed and confronted in our digital mediaverse. I present, if you will, a sort of antinarrative, an argument about the way in which we transform and interact with "nature" in reality and "nature" in the multitude of dialogical platforms that define our online personae. My show *I Can Haz Relational Dystopia?* is currently touring major museums around the world and was called "an unmitigated intellectual triumph" by *Feline Art Quarterly*. Now, if you'll excuse me, I am going to go pee in a box of sand in the kitchen.

Tabby Cat
Hartenstein,
Germany

PetCam

Fritz   •   Tabby Cat

Underscoring this beautiful scene is the understanding that summer will slowly decay into autumn, marching us to a cold, dead, and frozen winter. All struggle is futile in the face of time's scythe.

Fritz • Tabby Cat

PetCam

 Fritz • Tabby Cat

Hell is other cats.

PetCam

Fritz • Tabby Cat

PetCam

Fritz • Tabby Cat

PetCam

An interspecies peace offering. My heart says accept in good faith, my feline instincts say I should swat it out of her hand with my razor-sharp claws. Such is life.

Fritz • Tabby Cat

GUS

I am so friggin' anxious. I mean, it's not like my heart rate is calm and relaxed on a good day, but this is just too much pressure. Especially with that parrot just looking at me. What does he want? Parrots are basically dinosaurs, am I right? It's like a feathered T. rex just staring me down with his beady little pirate-loving eye. I CAN'T TAKE IT!!

Abyssinian
Guinea Pig
Poway, California

Okay, fine. Maybe he's thirty-five years old (that's like six hundred in guinea pig years!), and maybe he can squawk a few human words now and again. But he still eats out of a bowl on the floor like the rest of us.

I haven't moved in two hours. I'm just sitting here, silently shaking. Where did he go? I need a Xanax.

Gus • Abyssinian Guinea Pig

HAMLET & WALTER

The good thing about living our alternative pig lifestyle (in the suburbs rather than on a farm) is that: (a) Wally and I get to watch a lot of TV (I like reruns of *Hardcastle and McCormick*, he likes *Ellen*) and (b) we get snacks. *Lots* of snacks. It's funny, then, that in our photos you will see neither TV viewing nor snacks. We're good curators, I guess.

Miniature
Potbellied Pigs
San Diego, CA

#EmoBandAlbumCoverArt

Hamlet & Walter • Miniature Potbellied Pigs

Hamlet, nosing for clams. Oh, wait a second. Hamlet...? "Ham"-let...!
All these years together, and I just got that!

Hamlet & Walter • Miniature Potbellied Pigs

Here I am reenacting the climactic scene from *Planet of the Apes*. (Spoiler alert: we're going to add the Statue of Liberty in postproduction.)

PENNY

My photos—my art—it's really
all about the chickens, you know?
I'm a chicken, my friends are all
chickens, we all sleep in a chicken
coop, we hang out in a yard full of
other chickens....What did you
expect, photos of the monkey-flunkin'
Eiffel Tower? First thing I did when
I hatched, I bought a copy of Robert
Frank's *The Americans* on eBay.
Street photography speaks to me—
in my work, I want you to hear the
clucks; smell the chicken feed; and
really, truly, think about us chickens.
At the heart of every image I make
is that simple, age-old question:
Why do we cross the road? Wouldn't
you like to know.

PetCam

Penny • Blue Foot Chicken

Ha, ha, fatty!

I love the skywriting going on here. I can't read, but I'm pretty certain that it says "Cluck, cluck."

Penny • Blue Foot Chicken

Turkeys. The WORST.

Penny • Blue Foot Chicken

SCRAPPY

I love everyone I meet, but don't think I'm just a social butterfly. Even though every lap is a comfy bed for napping, I have ambitions. My dream job would be to shoot for the *SI* swimsuit issue. I'd like my shoot to be the first to feature a Mexican hairless as a cover model. It's time to break the species barrier, people.

Chihuahua
San Diego
California

PetCam

My philosophy is: practice random acts of snuggle.

Scrappy • Chihuahua

PetCam

 Scrappy • Chihuahua

Somebody should really talk to
this architect.

PetCam

VILLA

As head of my herd, and as I am, indeed, a bit type A, I admit that I mostly use my camera to check up on these other slacker goats I have to watch over. I do a monthly PowerPoint shaming presentation at the farm, in which I admonish any goat I catch on camera doing ungoatly activities. If you're not head butting someone or eating an old boot, you're not a goat worthy of the name.

Nera Verzasca
Goat

Münstertal,
Southern Black
Forest, Germany

PetCam

After a tough day, a field of grass. We work hard, and we play hard.

 Villa • Nera Verzasca Goat

XANDER

Ah, Tokyo! A photographer's town.
I love to take photos of bicycles,
shop windows, and well-manicured
scenes of domestic life. I also like
to follow my owner around the city as
if I were a dog and play fetch as if
I were a dog. They may say I'm a cat,
but I never let labels bring me down.

Manx Mix Cat
Tokyo, Japan

PetCam

I've been waiting for Keyboard Cat to show up for years. No luck.
I wish I knew how to Internet.

Xander • Manx Mix Cat

TIPS & RESOURCES

GETTING READY

- Check that your battery is fully charged and your memory card is empty before setting off.
- Start the automatic shutter just before you attach the camera, to avoid bothering your pet while fussing with the controls.
- Try using a specialized dog photo-harness to attach the camera to the top of your pup instead of hanging it from the collar. (These can be difficult to find locally but can be purchased online.)
- Be sure collars and harnesses are attached securely before letting your pet roam free, so you don't lose the camera.
- The camera's position affects the clarity of the photographs: adjusting the collar or harness a bit can greatly improve image quality.

PetCam

- Purchase a large memory card for your camera so you don't have to worry about running out of space.
- Use a faster-rated memory card with large capacity if you plan to set the camera to record at very short intervals (one or two seconds). If you use a slower-rated memory card, there may be a delay as the photos are saved to the card.
- Morning and late afternoon often provide optimal lighting conditions: the sun is low in the sky, colors are warm, shadows are deep, and there's the possibility of capturing interesting light flares.
- Images shot inside will usually be blurry or grainy unless there is a substantial amount of available light.
- Motion creates blurry photos; encourage your pet to stop and investigate subjects to increase clarity.
- If you're using a GoPro with Wi-Fi, you can use the GoPro app to control the camera with your phone. This is a great feature that works like a viewfinder, so you can see what the camera is seeing.

CREATIVE SUGGESTIONS

- If your pet enjoys the company of other animals, encourage social activity to capture portraits of your pet's buddies. The local dog park and beach are always good environments for interaction.
- To capture a variety of colors, textures, shapes, angles, and forms, visit settings that are visually rich, like flea markets, fairs, carnivals, sculpture gardens, playgrounds, or farms (as long as animal visitors are welcome).
- Document a vacation together by both taking photos.
- If your pet is facing the sun while using the camera, stand in front of the sun. Use your body to shade the camera and produce artistic silhouettes.
- Go for a walk with your pet at dusk or late at night and use a powerful flashlight to illuminate the scenery.
- If you plan to take photos for an hour or less, set the camera to take one photo every second. Yes, you will have many photos to sift through, but you will increase your odds of creating gems.

- Always make sure that the camera is comfortable for your pet—that it's not too heavy and that the animal is eager to participate in pet photography.
- The collar or harness you use to attach the equipment is equally as important as the camera. For safety, choose an adjustable collar with a quick-release function; be sure your pet is comfortable if s/he has never worn a collar before.
- Dedicate a separate collar to your pet's camera, so you're not attaching the camera to the collar your pup or cat wears every day.
- If you have more than one pet and/or camera, use color-coded collars to distinguish among cameras.

POSTSHOOTING TIPS

● Remove the collar or harness and camera as soon as your pet is done shooting.

● Don't get discouraged if you have to sort through hundreds of photographs before you find one incredible shot; image editing is part of the process—and part of the fun!

● Organize your photos in dated folders. Note dates and captions, so you can remember where you were and what you did.

● Divide your photos into two sets: favorites and outtakes.

● Set up a Flickr set and/or an Instagram account for your pet's photos and share images, ideas, and tips with other pet owners.

● Charge the battery as soon as you return home, so your equipment is good to go when you and your pet are ready to set off on your next adventure.

PetCam

One of the great things about PetCam photography is that you don't need a lot of gear to get started. Before you run out and buy a camera, though, it's important to know that not just any camera can work: you'll need a device that can take photos at timed intervals. Whichever camera you end up using, attach it to your pet securely, or you may wind up searching for it.

For the sake of simplicity, I've focused on two simple categories of camera: low-tech and high-tech options. There are other cameras available, but I've personally experimented with the three below.

1) INEXPENSIVE AND LOW-TECH

Low-tech cameras usually are lightweight, so they are appropriate for smaller animals (cats, small dogs, etc.). Image quality and resolution are what you would expect from a tiny camera: acceptable enough. The smaller file size makes it easy to share your images with others via email, text messages, and social media. For best results, use these cameras in daylight; photos captured indoors are often blurry, underexposed, and grainy, although I find that the effects created by these "lo-fi" cameras (image distortion, motion blur, and lens flare) can be quirky and appealing.

Mr. Lee's CatCam

2.1 x 1.6 x 1 in. (1 oz.)

It's called a CatCam, but owners of various animals, large and small, have chosen to explore PetCam photography with this little camera. (It's responsible for helping to create a fair share of the photographs in this collection.) German engineer Juergen Perthold invented the camera in 2007. He was curious about how his cat, Mr. Lee, spent his days, and at the time there wasn't a similar device on the market. The function settings are a bit tricky to navigate at first, but once you get the hang of it, it's a snap to use. You can set this camera to record images at intervals of seconds, minutes, or hours. It can record video and still photographs and includes a rechargeable battery, which can be fully charged with a USB cord. *mr-lee.com*.

Uncle Milton Nat Geo Wild Pet's Eye View Camera

3 x 2 x 1 in. (2.4 oz. with batteries)

Another affordable PetCam option, this camera operates on two AAA batteries and allows you to set the shutter at intervals of one, five, or fifteen minutes. (I typically program the shutter to record photographs as often as possible—e.g., one every minute—to increase the odds of capturing those star photographs.) *unclemilton.com/nat_geo_wild/wild_pets_eye_view_camera/*

2) EXPENSIVE AND HIGH-TECH

In the world of photography, you usually get what you pay for when it comes to optics, image sensor, and camera features. The best camera for your needs will depend on what you want to do with the images. Files generated from a small-megapixel camera cannot be enlarged with the sharpness and clarity of those created with a larger-megapixel camera, such as the GoPro. If you want to create prints that are 11 x 14 inches or larger, it's best to go the high-tech route. By spending a few extra dollars, you will expand your options and get better image quality.

GoPro

Camera with housing: 3 x 1 x 1.5 in. (4.8 oz.)

Even though the GoPro is small in size, it is a solid choice if you want to experiment with a more sophisticated camera right out of the box. The GoPro is impressive: the photos and videos are sharp and high quality, and the construction is durable. Keep in mind that this camera should never be attached to an animal too small to carry it. It is for large animals (big dogs, horses, cows, etc.). I highly recommend buying or making your own harness to secure it—for your animal's comfort and for clarity of image. (If not properly attached, the camera will sway to one side or another.) In addition, you must protect the camera's optics and electronics by keeping it within its housing and waterproof case whenever attaching it to your pet (who will inevitably test the integrity of your equipment). *gopro.com*.

Cooper: Photographer Cat

photographercat.com

The National Geographic & University of Georgia Kitty Cams (Crittercam) Project

kittycams.uga.edu/photovideo.html

Swiss Cow Photographers

cowcam.ch

ACKNOWLEDGMENTS

It's always easier to achieve our goals when we have some help from others. In writing this book, which is all about collaboration among people and pets, it became obvious to me how very interdependent we are. I came to realize that I sometimes take for granted the love that these furry and feathered friends give us, but I also learned that when people and animals work together as a team, great things can be achieved. I just wish I could speak dog so I could thank Fred for all his help. But I think deep down he knows that I'm grateful.

My sincere thanks go out to all the featured animals and their human companions: Abbott and Sarah Higgins; Astro, Scrappy, and Jennifer Phillips; Botty, with Sani Chan and Ho-Yin Leung; Casper, with Carla and Walter Reuben-Carbone; Chicken and Lisa Starr Goodin; Coulee and Wendy Devent; Fida, Lola, and their friends at cowcam.ch; Fiona, Penny, and the folks at Womach Ranch Farms; Fritz and Ramona Markstein; Gus and Annie Petersen; Villa and Marc Morell; Hamlet and Walter, with Mel and Ben Martinez; and Xander and Vanessa Miller.

Of course there are many other people who have helped pull this book together, and I know I couldn't have done it without them, either. First of all many thanks need to go out to my editors at Princeton Architectural Press, Sara Bader and Sara Stemen. I'm thankful to have people like Jay Sacher and Carson Berglund as my wordsmithing crew to help me polish the text until it shines. And, as I was a graphic designer for a good part of my life, I appreciate the talent and creativity that Elana Schlenker has put into the design and layout of this book. Of course, everyone has heard that saying "It takes a village"; I owe many thanks to the entire Princeton Architectural Press team for helping me bring this book to life. Since this is my second book it feels as though they're family now.

Thanks are due to the San Diego Humane Society and SPCA, as well as to Petco, which has had a major presence in my own pet community in San Diego.

Lastly I would like to thank my readers for buying and reading this book. I hope this book helps you create a positive relationship with your pet, which in turn leads to great times and amazing images.

CREDITS

Front cover photograph: Sara Bader. Casper appears courtesy of Carla and Walter Reuben-Carbone, On the Bluff Labradors (ontheblufflabradors.com). Casper is modeling a CatCam (mr-lee.com). 17: Sarah Higgins. 18-21: Abbott Higgins. 23-31; 116-121: Jennifer Phillips. 33-35: Sani Chan and Ho-Yin Leung. 37: Sara Bader. 38-39: Carla and Walter Reuben-Carbone and Casper. 41-45: Lisa Starr Goodin. Back cover, top center; 47-53: Wendy Devent, Paws on the Run (paws-on-the-run.ca). 55-59: cowcam.ch. Back cover, top left, bottom center, and bottom right; 61-69; 71-79; 95; 107-113; 115: Chris Keeney. Back cover, bottom left; 81-93: Ramona Markstein. 96-97: Annie Petersen. Back cover, top right; 99-105: Mel and Ben Martinez. 123-125: Marc Morell. 127-129: Vanessa Miller and Alexander "Xander" Miller (we miss you).